NIST Special Publication 800-67

Revision 1

NIST

**National Institute of
Standards and Technology**
Technology Administration
U.S. Department of Commerce

Recommendation for the Triple Data Encryption Algorithm (TDEA) Block Cipher

Revised January 2012

William C. Barker, Elaine Barker

INFORMATION SECURITY

Computer Security Division

Information Technology Laboratory

National Institute of Standards and Technology

Gaithersburg, MD 20899-8930

January 2012

U.S. DEPARTMENT OF COMMERCE
John Bryson, Secretary

**NATIONAL INSTITUTE OF STANDARDS AND
TECHNOLOGY**
*Patrick D. Gallagher. Under Secretary for Standards and
Technology and Director*

AUTHORITY

This document has been developed by the National Institute of Standards and Technology (NIST) in furtherance of its statutory responsibilities under the Federal Information Security Management Act (FISMA) of 2002, Public Law 107-347.

NIST is responsible for developing standards and guidelines, including minimum requirements, for providing adequate information security for all agency operations and assets, but such standards and guidelines **shall not** apply to national security systems.

This Recommendation has been prepared for use by federal agencies. It may be used by nongovernmental organizations on a voluntary basis and is not subject to copyright. (Attribution would be appreciated by NIST.)

Nothing in this document should be taken to contradict standards and guidelines made mandatory and binding on federal agencies by the Secretary of Commerce under statutory authority. Nor should this recommendation be interpreted as altering or superseding the existing authorities of the Secretary of Commerce, Director of the OMB, or any other Federal official.

Conformance testing for implementations of this Recommendation will be conducted within the framework of the Cryptographic Algorithm Validation Program (CAVP) and the Cryptographic Algorithm Module Program (CMVP). The requirements of this Recommendation are indicated by the word "**shall**." Some of these requirements may be out-of-scope for CAVP or CMVP validation testing, and thus are the responsibility of entities using, implementing, installing or configuring applications that incorporate this Recommendation.

Acknowledgements

The authors wish to thank their colleagues, who reviewed drafts of this document and contributed to its development. The authors also gratefully acknowledge and appreciate the many comments from the public and private sectors whose thoughtful and constructive comments improved the quality and usefulness of this publication.

Abstract

This publication specifies the Triple Data Encryption Algorithm (TDEA), including its primary component cryptographic engine, the Data Encryption Algorithm (DEA). When implemented in an SP 800-38-series-compliant mode of operation and in a FIPS 140-2-compliant cryptographic module, TDEA may be used by Federal organizations to protect sensitive unclassified data. Protection of data during transmission or while in storage may be necessary to maintain the confidentiality and integrity of the information represented by the data. This Recommendation defines the mathematical steps required to cryptographically protect data using TDEA and to subsequently process such protected data. TDEA is made available for use by Federal agencies within the context of a total security program consisting of physical security procedures, good information management practices, and computer system/network access controls.

Key words: block cipher, computer security, cryptography, data encryption algorithm, security, triple data encryption algorithm.

Foreward

The Triple Data Encryption Algorithm (TDEA) is an **approved** cryptographic algorithm as required by Federal Information Processing Standard (FIPS) 140-2, *Security Requirements for Cryptographic Modules*. TDEA specifies both the DEA cryptographic engine employed by TDEA and the TDEA algorithm itself.

This Recommendation provides a description of a mathematical algorithm for cryptographically protecting binary coded information (e.g., using encryption and authentication). The algorithm described in this recommendation specifies cryptographic operations that are based on a binary number called a key.

Authorized users of computer data cryptographically protected using TDEA must have the key that was used to protect the data in order to process the protected data. The cryptographic algorithm specified in this Recommendation is assumed to be commonly known among its users. The cryptographic security of the data depends on the security provided for the key used to protect the data.

Data that is determined by a responsible authority to be sensitive, data that has a high value, or data that represents a high value should be cryptographically protected if it is vulnerable to unauthorized disclosure or undetected modification during transmission or while in storage. A risk analysis should be performed under the direction of a responsible authority to determine potential threats. The costs of providing cryptographic protection using this Recommendation, as well as of alternative methods for providing this protection, should be projected. A responsible authority then should make a decision, based on these analyses, whether or not to use cryptographic protection and this recommendation.

DEA was originally specified in FIPS 46, *The Data Encryption Standard*, which became effective July 1977. It was reaffirmed in 1983, 1988, 1993, and 1999. The DEA has now been withdrawn. The use of DEA is permitted only as a component function of TDEA. This Recommendation applies to all Federal agencies, contractors of Federal agencies, or other organizations that process information (using a computer or telecommunications system) on behalf of the Federal Government to accomplish a Federal function. Each Federal agency or department may issue internal directives for the use of this recommendation by their operating units based on their data security requirement determinations.

With the withdrawal of the FIPS 46-3 standard (i.e., the final revision of FIPS 46), implementations of the DEA function are no longer authorized for protection of Federal government information.

Note: Through the year 2030[1], Triple DES (TDEA) and the FIPS 197 Advanced Encryption Standard (AES) will coexist as **approved** algorithms – thus, allowing for a gradual transition to AES. (The AES is another symmetric-based encryption standard approved by NIST.)

Implementations of the algorithm specified in this Recommendation may be covered by U.S. and foreign patents. Certain cryptographic devices and technical data regarding them are subject to Federal export controls. Exports of cryptographic modules implementing this algorithm and technical data regarding them must comply with these Federal regulations and be licensed by the Bureau of Export Administration of the U.S. Department of Commerce. Applicable Federal government export controls are specified in Title 15, Code of Federal Regulations (CFR) Part 740.17; Title 15, CFR Part 742; and Title 15, CFR Part 774, Category 5, Part 2.

---

[1] TDEA with Keying Option 2 (see Section 3) is **approved** for the protection of Federal government information only through the period of time specified in SP 800-131A. Recommendations regarding the use of Option 2 are contained in SP 800-57, Part 1.

Table of Contents

National Institute of Standards and Technology

Special Publication 800-67

SPECIFICATIONS FOR THE

TRIPLE DATA ENCRYPTION ALGORITHM (TDEA) BLOCK CIPHER

1. INTRODUCTION

This Recommendation specifies the Triple Data Encryption Algorithm (TDEA) block cipher. The TDEA block cipher includes a Data Encryption Algorithm (DEA) cryptographic engine (specified in Section 2) that is implemented as a component of TDEA (specified in Section 3). TDEA functions incorporating the DEA cryptographic engine **shall** be designed in such a way that they may be used in a computer system, storage facility, or network to provide cryptographic protection to binary coded data. The method of implementation will depend on the application and environment. TDEA implementations **shall** be subject to being tested and validated as accurately performing the transformations specified in the TDEA algorithm and in NIST Special Publication (SP) 800-38[2].

1.1 Applications

Cryptography is utilized in various applications and environments. The specific utilization of encryption and the implementation of TDEA[3] will be based on many factors particular to the computer system and its associated components. In general, cryptography is used to protect data while it is being communicated between two points or while it is stored in a medium vulnerable to physical theft or technical intrusion (e.g., hacker attacks). In the first case, the key must be available by the sender and receiver simultaneously during communication. In the second case, the key must be maintained and accessible for the duration of the storage period. NIST Special Publications (SP) 800-133 provides **approved** methods for generating cryptographic keys[4], and SP 800-57, Part 1[5], provides recommendations for managing cryptographic keys, including the keys used by the algorithm specified in this Recommendation.

---

[2] SP 800-38: *Recommendation for Block Cipher Modes of Operation - Methods and Techniques.*

[3] And the cryptographic engine that forms the basis for TDEA.

[4] SP 800-133: *Recommendation for Cryptographic Key Generation.*

[5] SP 800-57, Part 1: *Recommendation for Key Management: General.*

1.2 Modes of Using the TDEA

SP 800-38 describes modes of operation for the TDEA block cipher described in this Recommendation. These modes of operation are **approved** for the protection of Federal government information.

1.3 Organization

Section 2 of this Recommendation describes the DEA cryptographic engine employed by TDEA.

Section 3 of the Recommendation describes the basic TDEA algorithm.

Appendices are provided for DEA primitives, examples of encryption and decryption using the TDEA block cipher operation; a glossary of terms; a list of references; a list of requirements for entities installing, configuring and using TDEA; and a list of version changes.

2. DATA ENCRYPTION ALGORITHM CRYPTOGRAPHIC ENGINE

The DEA cryptographic engine is used by TDEA to cryptographically protect (e.g., encrypt) blocks of data consisting of 64 bits under the control of a 64-bit key[6]. Subsequent processing of the protected data (e.g., decryption) is accomplished using the same key as was used to protect the data. Each 64-bit key **shall** contain 56 bits that are randomly generated and used directly by the algorithm as key bits. The other eight bits, which are not used by the algorithm, may be used for error detection. The eight error-detecting bits are set to make the parity of each 8-bit byte of the key odd. That is, there is an odd number of "1"s in each 8-bit byte[7].

During each application of the DEA engine, a block is subjected to an initial permutation IP, then to a complex key-dependent computation and finally to a permutation that is the inverse of the initial permutation, IP^{-1}. The key-dependent computation can be simply defined in terms of a function f and a function KS, called the key schedule. The DEA engine can be run in two directions - as a forward transformation[8] and as an inverse transformation[9]. The two directions differ only by the order in which the bits of the key are used.

Descriptions of the forward and inverse transformations are provided below, followed by a definition of the function f in terms of primitive functions called by the selection functions S_i, and the permutation function P. Values for S_i, P and KS of the engine are contained in Appendix A.

The following notation is convenient: Given two blocks L and R of bits, LR denotes the block consisting of the bits of L followed by the bits of R. Since concatenation is associative, $B_1B_2...B_8$, for example, denotes the block consisting of the bits of byte B_1 followed by the bits of byte B_2...followed by the bits of byte B_8.

2.1 DEA Forward Transformation

A sketch of the forward transformation is given in **Figure 1**.

---

[6] Blocks are composed of bits numbered from left to right, i.e., the left-most bit of a block is bit one.

[7] Sometimes keys are generated in an encrypted form. A random 64-bit number is generated and defined to be the cipher formed by the encryption of a key using a key-encrypting key. In this case the parity bits of the encrypted key cannot be set until after the key is decrypted.

[8] Often called "encryption."

[9] Often called "decryption."

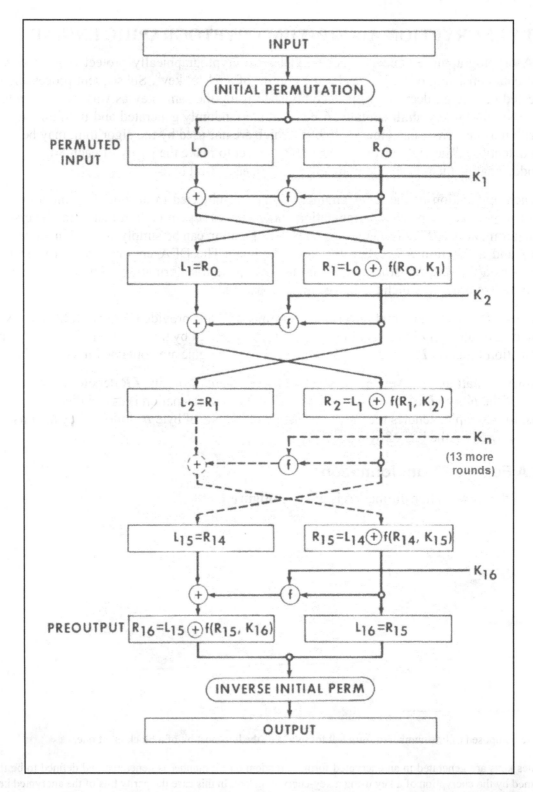

Figure 1. Forward Transformation of the DEA Cryptographic Engine

The 64 bits of the input block for the forward transformation are first subjected to the following permutation, called the initial permutation *IP*:

_IP_

58	50	42	34	26	18	10	2
60	52	44	36	28	20	12	4
62	54	46	38	30	22	14	6
64	56	48	40	32	24	16	8
57	49	41	33	25	17	9	1
59	51	43	35	27	19	11	3
61	53	45	37	29	21	13	5
63	55	47	39	31	23	15	7

That is, the permuted input has bit 58 of the input as its first bit, bit 50 as its second bit, and so on, with bit 7 as its last bit. The permuted input block is then the input to a complex key-dependent computation that is described below. The output of that computation, called the preoutput, is then subjected to the following permutation that is the inverse of the initial permutation:

_IP^1_

40	8	48	16	56	24	64	32
39	7	47	15	55	23	63	31
38	6	46	14	54	22	62	30
37	5	45	13	53	21	61	29
36	4	44	12	52	20	60	28
35	3	43	11	51	19	59	27
34	2	42	10	50	18	58	26
33	1	41	9	49	17	57	25

That is, the output of the algorithm has bit 40 of the preoutput block as its first bit, bit 8 as its second bit, and so on, until bit 25 of the preoutput block is the last bit of the output.

The key-dependent computation that uses the permuted input block as its input to produce the preoutput block consists, except for a final interchange of blocks, of 16 iterations of a calculation that is described below in terms of the function f. This function operates on two blocks, one of 32 bits and one of 48 bits, to produce a block of 32 bits.

Let the 64 bits of the input block to an iteration consist of a 32-bit block L, followed by a 32-bit block R. Using the notation defined above, the input block is then LR.

Let K be a block of 48 bits chosen from the 64-bit key. Then the output $L'R'$ of an iteration with input LR is defined by:

(1)
$$L' = R$$

$$R' = L \oplus f(R,K)$$

where $\oplus$ denotes bit-by-bit addition modulo 2 (also known as exclusive-or or XOR).

As remarked before, the input of the first iteration of the calculation is the permuted input block. If $L'R'$ is the output of the 16th iteration, then $R'L'$ is the preoutput block. At each iteration, a different block K of key bits is chosen from the 64-bit key designated by KEY.

With more notation, the iterations of the computation can be described in more detail. Let KS be a function that takes an integer n in the range from 1 to 16 and a 64-bit block KEY as input. The output of KS is a 48-bit block K_n that is a permuted selection of bits from KEY. That is:

(2)
$$K_n = KS(n, KEY)$$

with K_n determined by the bits in 48 distinct bit positions of KEY. KS is called the key schedule because the block K used in the n'th iteration of (1) is the block K_n determined by (2).

As before, let the permuted input block be LR. Finally, let L_0 and R_0 be respectively L and R, and let L_n and R_n be respectively L' and R' of (1) when L and R are respectively L_{n-1} and R_{n-1}, and K is K_n; that is, when n is in the range from 1 to 16,

(3)
$$L_n = R_{n-1}$$

$$R_n = L_{n-1} \oplus f(R_{n-1}, K_n)$$

The preoutput block is then $R_{16}L_{16}$.

The key schedule KS of the algorithm is described in detail in Appendix A. The key schedule produces the 16 K_n that are required for the algorithm.

2.2 DEA Inverse Transformation

The permutation IP^{-1} applied to the preoutput block is the inverse of the initial permutation IP

(4)
$$R = L'$$

$$L = R' \oplus f(L', K)$$

Consequently, to apply the inverse transformation, it is only necessary to apply the *very same algorithm to a block of the protected data produced by the forward transformation,* taking care that at each iteration of the computation, *the same block of key bits K is used* during the inverse transformation as was used during the forward transformation.

Using the notation of the previous section, this can be expressed by the equations:

(5)
$$R_{n-1} = L_n$$

$$L_{n-1} = R_n \oplus f(L_n, K_n)$$

where $R_{16}L_{16}$ is the permuted input block for the inverse transformation, and L_0R_0 is the preoutput block. That is, for the inverse transformation with $R_{16}L_{16}$ as the permuted input, K_{16} is used in the first iteration, K_{15} in the second, and so on, with K_1 used in the 16th iteration.

6

2.3 The Function f

A sketch of the calculation of $f(R, K)$ is given in **Figure 2**.

Let E denote a function that takes a block of 32 bits as input and yields a block of 48 bits as output. Let E be such that the 48 bits of its output, written as 8 blocks of 6 bits each, are obtained by selecting the bits in its inputs in order according to Table 1:

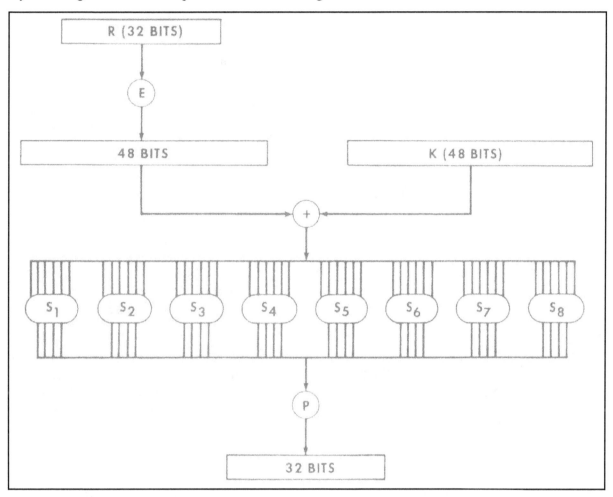

Figure 2. Calculation of f(R, K)

Table 1: *E* BIT-SELECTION TABLE

32	1	2	3	4	5
4	5	6	7	8	9
8	9	10	11	12	13
12	13	14	15	16	17

16	17	18	19	20	21
20	21	22	23	24	25
24	25	26	27	28	29
28	29	30	31	32	1

Thus, the first three bits of $E(R)$ are the bits in positions 32, 1 and 2 of R, while the last 2 bits of $E(R)$ are the bits in positions 32 and 1.

Each of the unique selection functions S_1, S_2,..., S_8, takes a 6-bit block as input and yields a 4-bit block as output and is illustrated by using Table 2. Table 2 contains S_1:

Table 2: S_1

Column Number

Row No.	0	1	2	3	4	5	6	7	8	9	10	11	12	13	14	15
0	14	4	13	1	2	15	11	8	3	10	6	12	5	9	0	7
1	0	15	7	4	14	2	13	1	10	6	12	11	9	5	3	8
2	4	1	14	8	13	6	2	11	15	12	9	7	3	10	5	0
3	15	12	8	2	4	9	1	7	5	11	3	14	10	0	6	13

If S_1 is the function defined in this table, and B is a block of 6 bits, then $S_1(B)$ is determined as follows: The first and last bits of B represent, in base 2, a number in the range 0 to 3. Let that number be i. The middle 4 bits of B represent, in base 2, a number in the range 0 to 15. Let that number be j. Using the table, look up the number in the i'th row and j'th column. It is a number in the range 0 to 15 and is uniquely represented by a 4-bit block. That block is the output $S_1(B)$ of S_1 for the input B. For example, for input 011011, the row is 01 (i.e., row 1), and the column is determined by 1101 (i.e., column 13). The number 5 appears in row 1, column 13, so the output is 0101.

Selection functions S_1, S_2,..., S_8 of the algorithm appear in Appendix A.

The permutation function P yields a 32-bit output from a 32-bit input by permuting the bits of the input block. Such a function is defined by Table 3:

Table 3: P

16	7	20	21
29	12	28	17
1	15	23	26

5	18	31	10
2	8	24	14
32	27	3	9
19	13	30	6
22	11	4	25

The output *P(L)* for the function *P* defined by this table is obtained from the input *L* by taking the 16th bit of *L* as the first bit of *P(L)*, the 7th bit as the second bit of *P(L)*, and so on until the 25th bit of *L* is taken as the 32nd bit of *P(L)*. The permutation function *P* of the algorithm is repeated in Appendix A.

Now let $S_1,..., S_8$ be eight distinct selection functions, let *P* be the permutation function, and let *E* be the function defined above.

To define *f(R, K)*, let $B_1,..., B_8$ be blocks of 6 bits each for which

(6) $B_1B_2...B_8 = K \oplus E(R)$

The block *f(R, K)* is then defined to be

(7) $P(S_1(B_1)S_2(B_2)...S_8(B_8))$

Thus, $K \oplus E(R)$ is first divided into the 8 blocks as indicated in (6). Then each B_i is taken as an input to S_i, and the 8 blocks $S_1(B_1), S_2(B_2),..., S_8(B_8)$ of 4 bits each are consolidated into a single block of 32 bits, which forms the input to *P*. The result (7) is then the output of the function *f* for the inputs *R* and *K*.

3. TRIPLE DATA ENCRYPTION ALGORITHM

3.1 Basic TDEA Forward and Inverse Cipher Operations

In this Recommendation, each TDEA forward and inverse cipher operation is a compound operation of the DEA forward and inverse transformations specified in Section 2.

A TDEA key consists of three keys for the cryptographic engine (*Key₁*, *Key₂* and *Key₃*); the three keys are also referred to as a key bundle (*KEY*). Two options for the selection of the keys in a key bundle are **approved**. Option 1, the preferred option, employs three unique keys (i.e. *Key₁*, *Key₂* and *Key₃*, where $Key_1 \neq Key_2$, $Key_2 \neq Key_3$, and $Key_3 \neq Key_1$). Option 2 employs two unique keys and a third key that is the same as the first key (i.e. *Key₁*, *Key₂* and *Key₃*, where $Key_1 \neq Key_2$ and $Key_3 = Key_1$). A key bundle **shall not** consist of three identical keys.

Let $F_{KeyX}(d)$ and $I_{KeyY}(d)$, respectively, represent the DEA forward and inverse transformations on data *d* using key bundle *KEY*. The following operations are used:

1. TDEA forward cipher operation: the transformation of a 64-bit block *d* into a 64-bit block *O* that is defined as follows:

$$O = F_{Key3}(I_{Key2}(F_{Key1}(d))).$$

2. TDEA inverse cipher operation: the transformation of a 64-bit block *d* into a 64-bit block *O* that is defined as follows:

$$O = I_{Key1}(F_{Key2}(I_{Key3}(d))).$$

3.2 TDEA Keying Options

This Recommendation specifies the following keying options for a TDEA key bundle *(Key₁, Key₂, Key₃)*

1. Keying Option 1: *Key₁*, *Key₂* and *Key₃* are unique keys (i.e., $Key_1 \neq Key_2$, $Key_2 \neq Key_3$, and $Key_3 \neq Key_1$);

2. Keying Option 2: K_1 and K_2 are unique keys (i.e., $Key_1 \neq Key_2$, and $Key_3 = Key_1$).

3.3 TDEA Modes of Operation

TDEA **shall** be implemented using one or more of the modes of operation specified in SP 800-38. These modes of operation are **approved** for the protection of Federal government sensitive, but unclassified information. Each of the modes employs the TDEA forward or inverse cipher operations as defined in Section 3.1. Note that the TDEA block cipher **shall** be used to provide cryptographic security only when used in an **approved** mode of operation.

3.4 Keys

The TDEA keys **shall** be managed in accordance with SP 800-57, Part 1. SP 800-57, Part 1 also specifies time frames during which the TDEA keying options may be used.

3.4.1 Key Requirements

For all TDEA modes of operation, three cryptographic keys (Key_1, Key_2, Key_3) define a TDEA key bundle. The bundle and the individual keys **shall**:

a. be kept secret;

b. be generated using an **approved** method[10] that is based on the output of an **approved** random bit generator[11];

c. be independent of other key bundles;

d. have integrity whereby each key in the bundle has not been altered in an unauthorized manner since the time it was generated, transmitted, or stored by an authorized entity;

e. be used in the appropriate order as specified by the particular mode;

f. be considered a fixed quantity in which an individual key cannot be manipulated while leaving the other two keys unchanged; and cannot be unbundled except for its designated purpose.

3.4.2 Weak Keys

There are a few keys that are considered weak for the DEA cryptographic engine. The use of weak keys can reduce the effective security afforded by TDEA and should be avoided. Keys that are considered weak are (in hexadecimal format):

- 01010101 01010101
- FEFEFEFE FEFEFEFE
- E0E0E0E0 F1F1F1F1
- 1F1F1F1F 0E0E0E0E

Note that the weak keys listed above and the semi-weak keys and the possibly weak keys listed below are expressed with odd parity, which is indicated in the rightmost bit of each byte.

Some pairs of keys encrypt plaintext to identical ciphertext and also should be avoided. These semi-weak keys are (in hexadecimal format):

- 011F011F010E010E and 1F011F010E010E01
- 01E001E001F101F1 and E001E001F101F101
- 01FE01FE01FE01FE and FE01FE01FE01FE01
- 1FE01FE00EF10EF1 and E01FE01FF10EF10E
- 1FFE1FFE0EFE0EFE and FE1FFE1FFE0EFE0E

---

[10] See SP 800-133.

[11] See SP 800-90 and FIPS 140-2, Annex C.

- E0FEE0FEF1FEF1FE and FEE0FEE0FEF1FEF1

There are also 48 keys that produce only four distinct subkeys (instead of 16) - these are called possibly weak keys and should be avoided. These possibly weak keys are (in hex):

01011F1F01010E0E	1F1F01010E0E0101	E0E01F1FF1F10E0E
0101E0E00101F1F1	1F1FE0E00E0EF1F1	E0E0FEFEF1F1FEFE
0101FEFE0101FEFE	1F1FFEFE0E0EFEFE	E0FE011FF1FE010E
011F1F01010E0E01	1FE001FE0EF101FE	E0FE1F01F1FE0E01
011FE0FE010EF1FE	1FE0E01F0EF1F10E	E0FEFEE0F1FEFEF1
011FFEE0010EFEF1	1FE0FE010EF1FE01	FE0101FEFE0101FE
01E01FFE01F10EFE	1FFE01E00EFE01F1	FE011FE0FE010EF1
FE01E01FFE01F10E	1FFEE0010EFEF101	FE1F01E0FE0E01F1
01E0E00101F1F101	1FFEFE1F0EFEFE0E	FE1FE001FE0EF101
01E0FE1F01F1FE0E	E00101E0F10101F1	FE1F1FFEFE0E0EFE
01FE1FE001FE0EF1	E0011FFEF1010EFE	FEE0011FFEF1010E
01FEE01F01FEF10E	E001FE1FF101FE0E	FEE01F01FEF10E01
01FEFE0101FEFE01	E01F01FEF10E01FE	FEE0E0FEFEF1F1FE
1F01011F0E01010E	E01F1FE0F10E0EF1	FEFE0101FEFE0101
1F01E0FE0E01F1FE	E01FFE01F10EFE01	FEFE1F1FFEFE0E0E
1F01FEE00E01FEF1	E0E00101F1F10101	FEFEE0E0FEFEF1F1

3.5 Usage Guidance

The security of TDEA is affected by the number of blocks processed with one key bundle. One key bundle **shall not** be used to process more than 2^{32} 64-bit data blocks when the keys conform to Keying Option 1 (see Section 3.2). When Keying Option 2 is used, the keys **shall not** be used to process more than 2^{20} blocks (see SP 800-131A).

APPENDIX A: PRIMITIVE FUNCTIONS FOR THE DATA ENCRYPTION ALGORITHM

The choice of the primitive functions **KS, S₁,...,S₈** and **P** is critical to the strength of the transformations resulting from the algorithm. The tables below specify the functions **S₁,..., S₈** and **P**. For the interpretation of the tables describing these functions, see the discussion in Section 2.

The primitive functions **S₁,..., S₈** are:

S_1

14	4	13	1	2	15	11	8	3	10	6	12	5	9	0	7
0	15	7	4	14	2	13	1	10	6	12	11	9	5	3	8
4	1	14	8	13	6	2	11	15	12	9	7	3	10	5	0
15	12	8	2	4	9	1	7	5	11	3	14	10	0	6	13

S_2

15	1	8	14	6	11	3	4	9	7	2	13	12	0	5	10
3	13	4	7	15	2	8	14	12	0	1	10	6	9	11	5
0	14	7	11	10	4	13	1	5	8	12	6	9	3	2	15
13	8	10	1	3	15	4	2	11	6	7	12	0	5	14	9

S_3

10	0	9	14	6	3	15	5	1	13	12	7	11	4	2	8
13	7	0	9	3	4	6	10	2	8	5	14	12	11	15	1
13	6	4	9	8	15	3	0	11	1	2	12	5	10	14	7
1	10	13	0	6	9	8	7	4	15	14	3	11	5	2	12

S_4

7	13	14	3	0	6	9	10	1	2	8	5	11	12	4	15
13	8	11	5	6	15	0	3	4	7	2	12	1	10	14	9
10	6	9	0	12	11	7	13	15	1	3	14	5	2	8	4
3	15	0	6	10	1	13	8	9	4	5	11	12	7	2	14

S_5

2	12	4	1	7	10	11	6	8	5	3	15	13	0	14	9
14	11	2	12	4	7	13	1	5	0	15	10	3	9	8	6

| 4 | 2 | 1 | 11 | 10 | 13 | 7 | 8 | 15 | 9 | 12 | 5 | 6 | 3 | 0 | 14 |
| 11 | 8 | 12 | 7 | 1 | 14 | 2 | 13 | 6 | 15 | 0 | 9 | 10 | 4 | 5 | 3 |

$\underline{S_6}$

12	1	10	15	9	2	6	8	0	13	3	4	14	7	5	11
10	15	4	2	7	12	9	5	6	1	13	14	0	11	3	8
9	14	15	5	2	8	12	3	7	0	4	10	1	13	11	6
4	3	2	12	9	5	15	10	11	14	1	7	6	0	8	13

$\underline{S_7}$

4	11	2	14	15	0	8	13	3	12	9	7	5	10	6	1
13	0	11	7	4	9	1	10	14	3	5	12	2	15	8	6
1	4	11	13	12	3	7	14	10	15	6	8	0	5	9	2
6	11	13	8	1	4	10	7	9	5	0	15	14	2	3	12

$\underline{S_8}$

13	2	8	4	6	15	11	1	10	9	3	14	5	0	12	7
1	15	13	8	10	3	7	4	12	5	6	11	0	14	9	2
7	11	4	1	9	12	14	2	0	6	10	13	15	3	5	8
2	1	14	7	4	10	8	13	15	12	9	0	3	5	6	11

The primitive function **P** is:

16	7	20	21
29	12	28	17
1	15	23	26
5	18	31	10
2	8	24	14
32	27	3	9
19	13	30	6
22	11	4	25

Recall that K_n, for $1 \leq n \leq 16$, is the block of 48 bits of the algorithm in (2). Hence, to describe **KS**, it is sufficient to describe the calculation of K_n from a key (**Key**$_i$) of the key bundle for $n = 1$, 2,..., 16. That calculation is illustrated in Figure 4. To complete the definition of **KS**, it is therefore sufficient to describe the two permuted choices, as well as the schedule of left shifts. One bit in each 8-bit byte of **Key**$_i$ may be utilized for error detection in key generation, distribution and storage. Bits 8, 16,..., 64 are for use in assuring that each byte is of odd parity. (Note that these eight parity bits have no effect on the operation of the algorithm.)

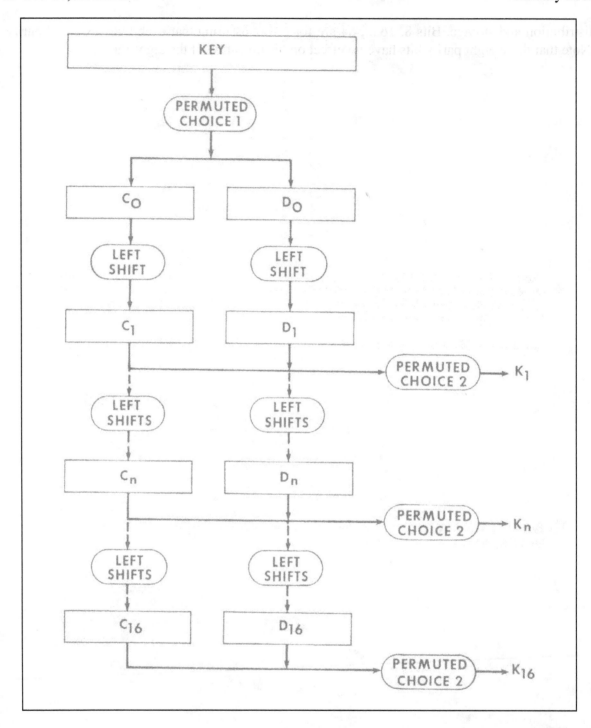

Figure 4: *Key Schedule Calculation*

Permuted choice 1 is determined by the following table:

PC-1

57	49	41	33	25	17	9
1	58	50	42	34	26	18
10	2	59	51	43	35	27
19	11	3	60	52	44	36
63	55	47	39	31	23	15
7	62	54	46	38	30	22
14	6	61	53	45	37	29
21	13	5	28	20	12	4

The table has been divided into two parts, with the first part determining how the bits of $C_{()}$ are chosen, and the second part determining how the bits of $D_{()}$ are chosen. The bits of Key_i are numbered 1 through 64. The bits of $C_{()}$ are respectively bits 57, 49, 41,..., 44 and 36 of Key_i, with the bits of $D_{()}$ being bits 63, 55, 47,..., 12 and 4 of Key_i.

With $C_{()}$ and $D_{()}$ defined, the blocks C_n and D_n are obtained from the blocks C_{n-1} and D_{n-1}, respectively, for $n = 1, 2,..., 16$, by adhering to the following schedule of left shifts of the individual blocks:

Iteration Number	Number of Left Shifts
1	1
2	1
3	2
4	2
5	2
6	2
7	2
8	2
9	1
10	2
11	2
12	2

13	2
14	2
15	2
16	1

For example, C_3 and D_3 are obtained from C_2 and D_2, respectively, by two left shifts, and C_{16} and D_{16} are obtained from C_{15} and D_{15}, respectively, by one left shift. In all cases, by a single left shift is meant a rotation of the bits one place to the left, so that after one left shift the bits in the 28 positions are the bits that were previously in positions 2, 3,..., 28, 1.

Permuted choice 2 is determined by the following table:

PC-2

14	17	11	24	1	5
3	28	15	6	21	10
23	19	12	4	26	8
16	7	27	20	13	2
41	52	31	37	47	55
30	40	51	45	33	48
44	49	39	56	34	53
46	42	50	36	29	32

Therefore, the first bit of K_n is the 14th bit of C_nD_n, the second bit of K_n is the 17th bit of C_nD_n, and so on, with the 47th bit of K_n as the 29th bit of C_nD_n, and the 48th bit of K_n as the 32nd bit of C_nD_n.

APPENDIX B: EXAMPLE OF TDEA FORWARD AND INVERSE CIPHER OPERATIONS

This Appendix presents an example that may be used when implementing the TDEA forward and inverse cipher operations. Appendices B.1 and B.2 provide an example of TDEA forward and inverse cipher operations in the Electronic Codebook (ECB) mode as specified in SP 800-38A.

In this example, all keys, plaintext and ciphertext are expressed in hexadecimal. The example uses three independent keys (Keying Option 1), which are:

Key_1 = 0123456789ABCDEF

Key_2 = 23456789ABCDEF01

Key_3 = 456789ABCDEF0123

The plaintext for the example is selected from the ASCII encoding of the phrase "The quick brown fox jumped over the lazy dog's back". The example employs the first 24 characters of the phrase (i.e., The quick brown fox jump).

The ASCII encoding of the above phrase is segmented as follows:

P_1	"The quic"	5468652071756663
P_2	"k brown "	6B2062726F776E20
P_3	"fox jump"	666F78206A756D70

B.1   TDEA Block Cipher Forward Cipher Operations - ECB Mode

In the example below, the input and output of the DEA cryptographic engine are given sequentially. At step 1, the input to DEA_1 is P_1, and the output of DEA_1 is "A28E91724C4BBA31". At step 2, the input to DEA_2 is the output of DEA_1, and the output of DEA_2 is "5A2EA7F983A2F53F". At step 3, the input to DEA_3 is the output of DEA_2, and the output of DEA_3 is "A826FD8CE53B855F". The output of DEA_3 is the ciphertext C_1.

P_1 = "The quic" = 5468652071756663

Transformation and key used	Input	Output
DEA_1 - F_{Key1}	5468652071756663	A28E91724C4BBA31
DEA_2 - I_{Key2}	A28E91724C4BBA31	5A2EA7F983A2F53F
DEA_3 - F_{Key3}	5A2EA7F983A2F53F	A826FD8CE53B855F

$C_1 = \text{A826FD8CE53B855F}$

During the second TDEA operation, the input is P_2, and the output after the three steps is ciphertext C_2.

P_2 = "k brown " = 6B2062726F776E20

Transformation and key used	Input	Output
DEA$_1$ - F$_{Key1}$	6B2062726F776E20	167E47EC24F71D63
DEA$_2$ – I$_{Key2}$	167E47EC24F71D63	EA141A7DD69701F0
DEA$_3$ – F$_{Key3}$	EA141A7DD69701F0	CCE21C8112256FE6

$C_2 = \text{CCE21C8112256FE6}$

During the third TDEA operation, the input is P_3, and the output after the three steps is ciphertext C_3.

P_3 = " fox jump" = 666F78206A756D70

Transformation and key used	Input	Output
DEA$_1$ – F$_{Key1}$	666F78206A756D70	2C1A917234425365
DEA$_2$ – I$_{Key2}$	2C1A917234425365	8059EE8212E22A79
DEA$_3$ – F$_{Key3}$	8059EE8212E22A79	68D5C05DD9B6B900

$C_3 = \text{68D5C05DD9B6B900}$

The resulting ciphertext is the concatenation of C_1, C_2 and C_3 (i.e., A826FD8CE53B855F CCE21C8112256FE6 68D5C05DD9B6B900).

B.2 TDEA Block Cipher Inverse Cipher Operation - ECB Mode

During inverse cipher operations in the ECB mode, the ciphertext C_1, C_2 and C_3 from Appendix B.1 are fed into the TDEA to produce the plaintext P_1, P_2 and P_3. The output of DEA$_3$ becomes the input to DEA$_2$, and the output of DEA$_2$ becomes the input to DEA$_1$.

$C_1 = \text{A826FD8CE53B855F}$

Transformation and key used	Input	Output

DEA$_3$ − I$_{Key3}$	A826FD8CE53B855F	5A2EA7F983A2F53F
DEA$_2$ − F$_{Key2}$	5A2EA7F983A2F53F	A28E91724C4BBA31
DEA$_1$ − I$_{Key1}$	A28E91724C4BBA31	5468652071756663

$P_1 = 5468652071756663 = $ "The quic".

$C_2 = CCE21C8112256FE6$

Transformation and key used	Input	Output
DEA$_3$ − I$_{Key3}$	CCE21C8112256FE6	EA141A7DD69701F0
DEA$_2$ − F$_{Key2}$	EA141A7DD69701F0	167E47EC24F71D63
DEA$_1$ − I$_{Key1}$	167E47EC24F71D63	6B2062726F776E20

$P_2 = 6B2062726F776E20 = $ "k brown ".

$C_3 = 68D5C05DD9B6B900$

Transformation and key used	Input	Output
DEA$_3$ − I$_{Key3}$	68D5C05DD9B6B900	8059EE8212E22A79
DEA$_2$ − F$_{Key2}$	8059EE8212E22A79	2C1A917234425365
DEA$_1$ − I$_{Key1}$	2C1A917234425365	666F78206A756D70

$P_3 = 666F78206A756D70 = $ "fox jump".

The plaintext is the ASCII encoding of "The quick brown fox jump".

APPENDIX C: GLOSSARY

Approved	FIPS-approved or NIST-recommended: an algorithm or technique that is either 1) specified in a FIPS or NIST Recommendation, or 2) adopted in a FIPS or NIST Recommendation.
Authentication	Provides assurance of the authenticity and, therefore, the integrity of data.
Bit	A binary digit having a value of zero or one.
Block	In this Recommendation, a binary string, for example, a plaintext or a ciphertext, is segmented with a given length. Each segment is called a block. Data is processed block by block, from left to right.
Block Cipher Algorithm	A family of functions and their inverses that is parameterized by a cryptographic key; the function maps bit strings of a fixed length to bit strings of the same length.
Byte	A group of eight bits that is treated either as a single entity or as an array of eight individual bits.
Ciphertext	Encrypted (enciphered) data.
Cryptographic Key	A parameter that determines the transformation using DEA and TDEA forward and inverse operations.
Data Encryption Algorithm	The DEA cryptographic engine that is used by the Triple Data Encryption Algorithm (TDEA).
Decryption	The process of transforming ciphertext into plaintext.
Encryption	The process of transforming plaintext into ciphertext.
Exclusive-OR	The bit-by-bit modulo 2 addition of binary vectors of equal length.
FIPS	Federal Information Processing Standard.
Forward Cipher Operation/Forward Transformation	One of the two functions of the block cipher algorithm that is determined by the choice of a cryptographic key. The term "forward cipher operation" is used for TDEA, while the term "forward transformation" is used for DEA.

Inverse Cipher Operation/Inverse Transformation	The block cipher algorithm function that is the inverse of the forward cipher function. The term "inverse cipher operation" is used for TDEA, while the term "inverse transformation" is used for DEA.
Key	See cryptographic key.
Key Bundle	The three cryptographic keys (Key_1, Key_2, Key_3) that are used with a TDEA mode.
Plaintext	Intelligible data that has meaning and can be read or acted upon without the application of decryption. Also known as cleartext.

APPENDIX D: REFERENCES

Federal information Processing Standards (FIPS) and NIST Special Publications (SPs) are available at http://csrc.nist.gov/publications/.

FIPS 140-2	*Security Requirements for Cryptographic Modules*, May 25, 2001.
FIPS 140-2, Annex C	*Approved Random Number Generators*, June 14, 2011; available at http://csrc.nist.gov/groups/STM/cmvp/standards.html.
FIPS 197	*Advanced Encryption Standard*, November 2001.
SP 800-20	*Modes of Operation Validation System for the Triple Data Encryption Algorithm (TMOVS): Requirements and Procedures*, SP 800-20, April 2000 Revision.
SP 800-38A	*Recommendation for Block Cipher Modes of Operation, Methods and Techniques*, December 2001.
SP 800-38A Addendum	*Recommendation for Block Cipher Modes of Operation: Three Variants of Ciphertext Stealing for CBC Mode*, October 2010.
SP 800-38B	*Recommendation for Block Cipher Modes of Operation: The CMAC Mode for Authentication*, May 2005.
SP 800-57, Part 1	*Recommendation for Key Management*, March 2007.
SP 800-90	SP 800-90A: *Recommendation for Random Number Generation Using Deterministic Random Bit Generators*, Draft Revision, May 2011. SP 800-90C: Recommendation for Random Bit Generator (RBG) Constructions, Draft.
SP 800-131A	*Transitions: Recommendation for Transitioning the Use of Cryptographic Algorithms and Key Lengths*, January 2011.
SP 800-133	*Recommendation for Cryptographic Key Generation*, Draft.

APPENDIX E: CONFORMANCE REQUIREMENTS FOR INSTALLATION, CONFIGURATION AND USE

Conformance to many of the requirements in this Recommendation are the responsibility of entities installing, configuring or using applications or protocols that incorporate this Recommendation. These requirements include the following:

Section	Requirement
1	TDEA functions incorporating the DEA cryptographic engine **shall** be designed in such a way that they may be used in a computer system, storage facility, or network to provide cryptographic protection to binary coded data.
2	Each 64-bit key **shall** contain 56 bits that are randomly generated and used directly by the algorithm as key bits.
3.1	A key bundle **shall not** consist of three identical keys.
3.3	Note that the TDEA block cipher **shall** be used to provide cryptographic security only when used in an **approved** mode of operation.
3.4	The TDEA keys **shall** be managed in accordance with NIST Special Publication (SP) 800-57, Part 1.
3.4	The following specifications for keys **shall** be met in implementing the TDEA modes of operation.
3.4.1	The bundle and the individual keys **shall**: a. be kept secret; b. be generated using an **approved** method[12] that is based on the output of an **approved** random bit generator[13]; c. be independent of other key bundles; d. have integrity whereby each key in the bundle has not been altered in an unauthorized manner since the time it was generated, transmitted, or stored by an authorized source; e. be used in the appropriate order as specified by the particular mode; f. be considered a fixed quantity in which an individual key cannot be manipulated while leaving the other two keys unchanged; and cannot be unbundled except for its designated purpose.
3.5	One key bundle **shall not** be used to process more than 2^{32} 64-bit data blocks when the keys conform to Keying Option 1
3.5	When Keying Option 2 is used, the keys **shall not** be used to process more than 2^{20} blocks (see [SP 800-131A]).

---

[12] See SP 800-133.

[13] See SP 800-90 and FIPS 140-2, Annex C.

APPENDIX F: CHANGES

Version 1.1 modified the list of weak keys in Section 3.4.2, correcting the third and fourth weak keys in the list. In addition, a note was inserted that the actual values of the parity bits were ignored when listing the weak and semi-weak keys.

In version 1.2, the following non-editorial modifications have been made:

1. The authority section was updated, primarily to include a paragraph about validation testing.

2. References to American National Standard X9.52, *Triple Data Encryption Algorithm Modes Of Operation*, have been removed, since the standard was withdrawn.

3. Various parts of SP 800-38 have been referenced: SP 800-90 and FIPS 140-2, Annex C, have been referenced for random bit generators; SP 800-131A has been referenced for the transition away from two-key TDEA; and SP 800-133 has been referenced for key generation.

4. The previous Section 1.1, *Basis*, was removed, since the information is provided in the Authority section.

5. The previous Section 1.2, *Applicability*, was removed.

6. In Table 3 of Section 2.3, the third entry in the first row was corrected to be "20."

7. In Section 3.1, the relationship of the acceptable keys used for TDEA has been further clarified.

8. In Section 3.5, the "should not" in the statement "One key bundle should not be used to process more than 2^{32} 64-bit data blocks when the keys conform to Keying Option 1…" has been changed to "**shall not.**"

9. In Section 3.4.1, line 2, the "must" was changed to "**shall.**"

10. In Section 3.5, guidance for the use of Keying Options 1 and 2 was further clarified. In addition, the "should not" in the statement "One key bundle should not be used to process more than 2^{32} 64-bit data blocks when the keys conform to Keying Option 1…" has been changed to "**shall not.**"

11. In Appendix D, additional references were provided for SP 800-131A and SP 800-133.

12. Appendix E was added to identify requirements that are the responsibility of entities that install, configure or use applications or protocols that incorporate TDEA.

www.ingramcontent.com/pod-product-compliance
Lightning Source LLC
Chambersburg PA
CBHW060513060326
40689CB00020B/4728